THE SNOT BOOK

A BOOK FOR CHILDREN TO ENJOY AND LEARN ABOUT NOSE GOOP, MUCUS, AND OTHER CURIOUS FACTS

ROUNDED SPECS PUBLISHING
978-1-952343-02-5

Story & Art by MARK BACERA

Look! It's **snotty Sonny**.

Usually, Sonny's quite the snob, but today it seems like something's off.

He's reaching for a tissue pack.
Looks like he has a case of the sniffles.

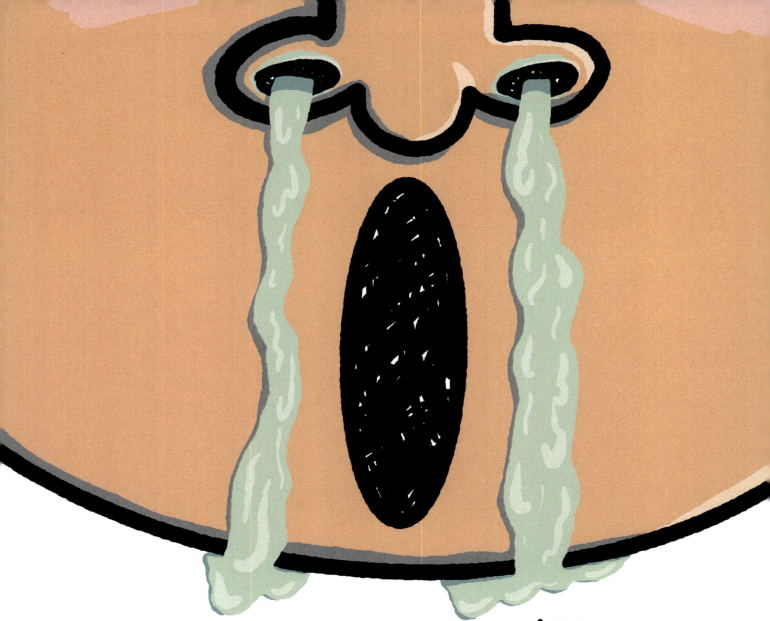

He **snorts** and he sniffs,
But the stuff doesn't stay in.

But wait! This doesn't seem right…

Something strange is coming out!

It's a **SN...**

Something else is coming out!

It's **SN**...

SNAP PEAS!
Again, this isn't right.
So, give it a wipe.

Something else is coming out!

It's a **SN**...

SNEAKER!
Again, this isn't right.
So, give it a wipe.

Something else is coming out!

It's a **SN**...

SNAKE!
Again, this isn't right.
So, give it a wipe.

Something else is coming out!

It's a **SN**...

Something else is coming out!

It's a **SN**...

Something else is coming out!

It's a **SN**...

SNOW LEOPARD!
Again, this isn't right. So, give it a wipe.

Something else is coming out!

It's a **SN**...

Something else is coming out!

It's a **SN**...

SNAPPING TURTLE!
Again, this isn't right. So, give it a wipe.

Something else is coming out!

It's a **SN**…

SNEAKY NINJA!
And again, this isn't right.
So, give it a wipe.

Oh!
What's this?

Something else is coming out!

Wait. Could it actually be?

Sonny **blows** and something **dances** in the wind.

He blows and he blows.

This is it! It's SN...

Wipe it off,
throw it away,
and wash your hands.

Good job Sonny!

Hey, it's me Dr. Boogers!
I hope you enjoyed Sonny's silly story.
Obviously all the crazy stuff was **snot** real!

(Hehe, I'm so punny!)

Next, I'll teach you a bit about **snot**.

Take a look at this picture.
Can you guess who it is?

Yep, that's me when I was younger!

Ahhh a younger, fitter, and more handsome Dr. Boogers—with hair as well!

The job of mucus is to act as a barrier to prevent things like dust, allergens, bacteria, germs, or viruses from getting inside the body.

You can think of them as little slippery soliders or even security guards!

To take care of our nasal warriors, make sure to drink a good amount of liquids.

Also, although mucus is good, don't worry about blowing them out. If you've noticed them, it means they've already completed their missions.

You've probably noticed that **snot** come in different **COLORS**.

The color of your **snot** can actually tell you if you're healthy, sick, or have other stuff stuck in your nose!

Let's take a look at what each color means.

CLEAR

You're in the clear—everything is totally fine.

If your nose gunk is clear, be happy!

WHITE or CLOUDY

You have congestion: Your snot is a little thicker because it has lost some moisture and because the insides of your nose are inflamed and swollen.

All of this points to a cold, infection, or an allergy.

If your snot is this color, you should tell a parent!

YELLOW

Your cold or infection is getting worse. Your body is sending more white blood cells (helpers in your body) to fight your illness.

It's difficult to explain, but the all these helpers gathering in your nose leaves your snot with a yellow tint.

Since yellow snot is worse than white, my suggestion is the same—tell a parent!

GREEN

This color is a sign that your body is working super hard to fight off your sickness.

More white blood cells are being sent to fight and this leads to an even darker color.

If you have a fever, feel like throwing up, or if this green snot lasts longer than 12 days, you should definitely see a doctor!

PINK or RED

This is a sign that there's blood in your mucus.

This could have happened because of dryness, irritation, or picking your nose too much (bad finger)!

If the bleeding doesn't stop, or if it is in addition to cold symptoms, you should certainly tell a parent.

BROWN

This could also be due to blood—dried blood, that is.

Another possibility is that a lot of smog or dirt went into your nose.

If it continues for a long time, tell a parent.

Whatever color your snot, be sure to blow your nose with a tissue.

Germs can live for several hours on tissues however, so don't forget to throw it away as soon as possible!

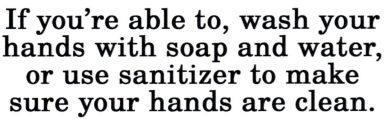

If you're able to, wash your hands with soap and water, or use sanitizer to make sure your hands are clean.

Practicing good hygiene, like cleaning your hands often, prevents those yucky germs, viruses, and bacteria from spreading to other people!

There's always more to say, but let's call it a day!

To review, keep your mucus happy by staying hydrated. Also when you blow your nose it's *always* good practice to clean your hands afterward.

Remember, if the color is very different from usual—tell a parent!

Smell you later!

The End

The Booger Book
A Book for Children to Enjoy Learning About Dried-up Mucus

Story and art by Mark Bacera

ISBN 978-1-952343-02-5

Copyright © 2020
Mark Bacera and
Rounded Specs Publishing LLC

www.roundedspecspublishing.com
FB.me/roundedspecspublishing
Instagram:
@roundedspecspublishing

About the Author

Mark Bacera is a bestselling author and released his first children's book called The Poo Poo Book (also the first book in the Bewildering Body series) in 2018. Since then, he has created several other titles.

The author lives in western Japan with his wonderful wife & daughter who also participate in the creative process and making of these books.

Amazon Author Page:
www.amazon.com/
mark-bacera/e/B0198EHT0M

Email:
mark@roundedspecs
publishing.com

*Authors love reviews!
To leave one, visit:*
www.amazon.com/dp/
B089Q8RMQN

Other Books by Mark

- The Poo Poo Book
- The Belly Button Book
- The Fart Book
- The Booger Book
- The Stinky Feet Book
- The Ear Wax Book
- The Sweat Book
- The Tear Book
- The Spit Book
- Baby Poop
- A Naughty Kid's Christmas ABC Story
- I'm an Alien-Vampire and I'm Proud of It!

Other Books by Rounded Specs

- A Day With Mae
- Ame the Cat
- Ame Goes to Japan
- Ame Goes to Hawaii
- Ame Goes to the North Pole
- Ame Goes to Egypt
- Ame Goes to the Zoo
- Ame's First Christmas
- Ame's Cafe
- Fashionable Animals
- What in the World Could it Be?

Please note that some of the above titles have yet to be published. To support us and be notified when new books are in the works and released, send us an email at info@roundedspecspublishing.com

Made in the USA
Monee, IL
19 March 2022